Johnson Publishing Company, Inc.

Chicago   1972

the Soul of Christmas

By Helen King
Illustrations by Fred Anderson

Juv
FIC
Cop. 3

It was nearly Christmas and Mama was helping the five kids and Daddy get dressed up in their warmest clothes so they could go and pick out a Christmas tree.

The kids loved Christmas—not just because they got toys and presents, but because Mama and Daddy were so happy and laughing all the time.

Mama waved to them when they got on the elevator. Some of the people on the elevator had packages and one lady had a bag with bright, shiny paper and colored ribbons on it.

The kid's hearts were pounding with excitement and happy thoughts kept dancing around in their stomachs. Daddy told Little Brother for the thousandth time to tie his shoelaces, but this time Daddy didn't seem to mind at all.

Outside, it was getting dark and the snowflakes fell like torn pieces of white paper. The children tried to catch snowflakes on their tongues. All the buildings were draped with snow and you couldn't even see the stars for the snowflakes. Daddy hustled them all into the Old Ford—all except Baby Junior who helped Daddy scrape snow off the car windows. Finally Daddy got the car warmed up and they were on their way.

"There're some trees!" Jeanie shouted.

"Nope, not there," said Daddy, "the trees there cost too much." They drove past lots of places and lots of people before Daddy finally got to the place where he wanted to buy a tree. Little Brother's shoestrings had come untied again and when he got out of the car he tripped and fell flat on his face in the snow.

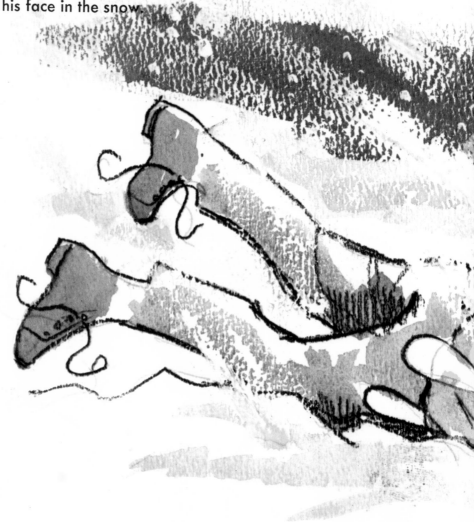

Even then, Daddy didn't get mad and just laughed and said, "One of these days those shoestrings are gonna put you in the hospital!" All the other kids giggled while Little Brother brushed big wads of snow off his face and coat. Then Little Brother punched Baby Junior who was laughing harder than anybody else. Well, Baby Junior was the oldest, so he just punched Little Brother right back, Daddy stopped walking and gave them both a hard look and everybody went over to where the trees were.

The tree man stood by a little wood-burning stove, warming his hands.

"Hey there, James," the tree man said to Daddy.

"Hey there," Daddy answered. "How's business?"

"Can't complain," said the tree man and the kids ran all over the big lot looking for trees.

There were fat ones and skinny ones and tall ones and short ones and Baby Junior wondered if there were enough people in the world to buy all those trees!

Daddy let everybody pick his favorite and said they would all vote on which one of the five trees they would buy. The tree man lined up the five trees. Finally, they voted on a tall, fat one with long branches.

Daddy and the tree man had to tie it to the top of the car because it wouldn't fit inside. On the way home Daddy let them sing Christmas carols, and when they got home the kids made snowballs and tracked in the snow while Daddy untied the tree.

It was a tight squeeze in the elevator with the tree, and
the tree kind of stuck if you got too near, but nobody
seemed to mind.

"Wow!" said Mama, opening the door for all of them. "That's the biggest, prettiest tree we've ever had."

She said that every year, but it always made Daddy smile when he heard it.

Mama had put up the old tree stand that they'd had since Jeanie was a baby and Daddy was putting up the tree with his gloves on so the needles wouldn't stick to his hands. Two times the tree seemed like it was going to fall and the kids all squealed, but finally the tree stood tall and straight.

Mama made some popcorn balls out of popcorn and syrup and the kids hung them on the tree. Little Brother made snowflakes out of colored paper and sprinkled some glitter on some glue and hung those on. Daddy was the only one who knew how to make a star, so he drew it and Mama cut it from a piece of aluminum foil and Daddy put it on the very top branch. They put on the tinsel left from last year and Mama draped an old sheet around the bottom. Daddy had bought some new lights that went on and off all by themselves and when they were finished Mama said: "This is the best-looking tree we've ever decorated."

The kids got so excited they started screaming and rolling around on the floor, so Mama decided it was time for everybody to go to bed.

The next day Mama gave everybody fifty cents apiece to buy presents. Baby Junior was the oldest and he was in charge and they all went to the novelty store two blocks from their house. Mama had taught them how to shop with fifty cents and she always reminded them: "It's not how *much* you spend, it's the thought!"

It was fun shopping.

There was a Santa Claus in the store and all the kids sat on his knee and told him what they wanted. All except Little Carolyn. She was only three and she was still a little scared of Santa Claus, but Santa gave her a free candy cane anyway.

Everybody had to keep the others from seeing what they
had bought so the presents would be a surprise. Jeanie
had to help Little Carolyn.

They bought ten cent coloring books and colored pencils and erasers and five cent peppermint sticks. And each one of them gave their leftover money to Baby Junior like always, and he bought Mama a lacy pink handkerchief and Daddy a white handkerchief with "J" on it for James. Nobody bought themselves anything because they knew they would get a lot of presents on Christmas Day, and that was only two days away!

That night when the kids were supposed to be sleeping, Mama and Daddy had a grown-up party. Baby Junior was the only one awake. He was real excited that night anyway, about more than Christmas. Their auntie had bought them two bunk beds at the rummage sale and Baby Junior didn't have to sleep with Little Brother anymore. Baby

Junior was real happy about that because Little Brother kicked people and sometimes even wet the bed! The girls got one of the bunk beds in their room too. Now everybody had their own bed and Jeanie got to sleep all by herself in a twin bed.

Baby Junior lay there listening to the grownups laughing. His favorite Marvin Gaye record was playing and finally Baby Junior got out of bed and crawled over to the door. He opened it a little and he could see Mama all dressed up in the pink dress Daddy liked so much.

Mama and Daddy were dancing and Baby Junior lay down with his hands under his chin and kept time to the music with his toes.

The last thing he remembered was hearing Isaac Hayes singing.

When Baby Junior woke up in the morning, Mama was standing over him.

"What in the world are you doing on the floor, boy?" she asked.

Baby Junior jumped up and ran back to his bed. He was sure he was going to get a whipping, so he covered up his head. "I should give you a good one," Mama said, pulling the covers off him, "But it's Christmas Eve," she said with a smile, "and I don't give whippings on Christmas Eve." Boy!! Was Baby Junior glad of that!

Mama went shopping for the Christmas turkey that day while the kids stayed home with Daddy and cleaned the house. Daddy mopped and waxed all the floors and the kids cleaned their rooms and straightened up the living room.

Mama and the delivery boy came home with five bags of groceries. The kids helped unpack. There were nuts in the

shell, oranges, apples, hard candy, Christmas wrapping paper, ribbon, sweet potatoes, greens, and the biggest, fattest turkey ever!

The kids all got to wrap the presents they had bought for each other, and while Baby Junior was putting the leftover ribbon and wrappings away, he thought he saw a toy box back in the corner of the closet.

He was just about to get a better look when Mama yelled from the kitchen, "Come take out the trash, Baby Junior, and get out of that closet."

Boy! It sure was funny how Mama could read his mind sometimes.

That night, all the children took their baths early and Mama let them stay up in their pajamas to watch *How the Grinch Stole Christmas* on television.

They could smell Mama's sweet potato pies and the turkey cooking.

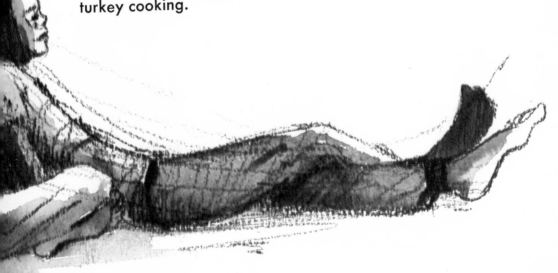

Daddy went out for a beer with his friend.

And perhaps the kids would have got to stay up late but
Little Brother sneaked and ate two of the popcorn balls
off the Christmas tree and Mama said it was time for bed.
It was almost time for Santa Claus anyway, she said.

"Where does Santa Claus get the money for presents for
kids all over the world?" Jeanie asked.

"Mamas and Daddys give him money," Mama said.
"Now go to sleep before he catches you awake.

"How come we never hear him?" Marilyn asked.

"Because he's a magic man," Mama answered, "and no
one can hear his footsteps."

"Do Mamas and Daddys ever get to see him," Jeanie
asked.

"Oh yes," said Mama. "We have to pay him!"
"Now go to sleep!"

Well, finally it was Christmas Day!

Little Carolyn and Mama and Daddy were still asleep when the others got up to see their gifts. Jeanie got a "Julia" doll that had two extra dresses. Baby Junior got a "Hot Wheels" set. Marilyn got a baby doll that wet. Little Brother got a set of tiny cars, and Carolyn got a baby doll too. Everybody got some underwear from Auntie and a stocking filled with candy!

They made so much noise that Mama and Daddy woke up and so did Little Carolyn. Mama got a beautiful blue gown from Daddy, and Daddy got a black shirt from Mama that had a white stripe across the middle.

The kids were just about to open the presents they had bought for each other when someone knocked on the door. It was the neighbor down the hall, and she had a worried look on her face.

Daddy told her to sit down on the couch.

"My kids aren't up yet," she told Mama and Daddy. "My husband was supposed to bring their toys last night, but he had a car accident and he's at the hospital."

The neighbor looked like she was going to cry. Mama put her arm round her and said,

"Well, we've got something extra, I think.

"They're not much."

"Oh no," said the neighbor. "I don't want to take your kids' stuff, but if I can borrow a few dollars I can still run to the novelty store. It's open till noon."

"Nope," said Daddy. "You just rest yourself. We've got stuff here."

Daddy got up from the couch and took all the kids into Baby Junior and Little Brother's room. The kids all sat down kind of sadly. They really didn't want to give up anything, and none of them even liked the neighbor's boy, Charles, because he was always starting fights.

"Do you remember where Christmas came from?" Daddy asked.

Nobody answered.

They kept their heads down, all except Little Carolyn who didn't know what was going on anyhow.

"Well, it's about Our Lord," Daddy continued. "And He was born on this day. And people brought Him presents because He was the Lord and that was something special because when the Lord got to be a grown man He gave His life so all the people could be free."

"Free from what?" asked Little Brother.

"Free from a mean king who kept them all slaves," said Daddy.

"Slaves like black people once were," asked Baby Junior, who had heard about slavery in school.

"Yes, like black people were once slaves," said Daddy. "So Christmas is really about giving and helping other people," he added. "Now all of you have presents already and you haven't even opened the ones you bought for each other, so I think we'll give those to the neighbor children since they don't have anything. And everybody should have something for Christmas."

"I hate to give up things," Little Brother complained. "Besides I don't even like Charles. He's always starting fights . . . and one time his sister pushed Carolyn backwards in the sandbox!"

"Well, maybe we should talk to them about that," said Daddy, "but they're still people like all of us, and how would you feel if you didn't get anything for Christmas and your Daddy was in the hospital and your Mama was about to cry?"

The kids all agreed that those were pretty bad things to have happen on Christmas, so they said they would give up the presents they had bought for each other. Little Carolyn didn't know the difference anyhow.

Even though the kids didn't feel too pleased about it at first, their hearts somehow felt good when they saw how happy Charles and his sister were to get the presents.

Charles said he was sorry about the fights without anyone even asking.

Baby Junior let Charles play with his "Hot Wheels" set and Little Brother gave him one of the seven little cars.

The neighbors stayed to dinner and Daddy took out the homemade wine for the grown-ups.

Baby Junior was ten so he got to taste the wine.

The kids had lots of fun playing with Charles and his sister and when Mama said it was the best Christmas she could remember, everybody had to agree!